BUDDHA

Mason Crest Publishers, Inc.
370 Reed Road
Broomall, Pennsylvania 19008
866-MCP-BOOK (toll free)

Illustrations copyright © 1999 Paolo D'Altan
Published in association with Grimm Press
        Ltd., Taiwan
Printed in Taiwan.

1 3 5 7 9 8 6 4 2

Library of Congress Cataloging-in-Publication
        Data:
on file at the Library of Congress.

ISBN 1-59084-137-9
ISBN 1-59084-133-6 (series)

Great Names

BUDDHA

Mason Crest Publishers

Philadelphia

About 2,500 years ago in the northeast of India, a great sage was born. People called him "Buddha," which meant "the enlightened one."

Buddha's father, Sudhodhana, was the maharajah or chieftain of the Sakyu tribe. The Sakyus lived in a region called Kapilavastu, which is now part of southern Nepal. The city of Kapilavastu was built high on top of a mountain. From a distance, it looked as if it were floating among the clouds.

Buddha's mother was the maharajanhee. Her name was Maya. It was said that she dreamed one night of a white elephant, which flew down from the moonlit sky into her bed, and that not long afterward she discovered she was pregnant.

Nine months later, on a journey to her parents' home, Maya

gave birth to a baby boy under a tree beside the road. He was given the name Siddhartha. This boy would become the Buddha.

Legend has it that after Siddhartha was born, a holy man came to visit Sudhodhana. He saw Siddhartha, and said, "Your Highness, your son is going to be a great saint. He will abandon the crown and become a monk.

What a pity I am too old to hear his wise teachings."

When he heard this, Sudhodhana became very worried that his son would leave him. But Siddhartha grew into a fine young prince. He was very good at everything, from martial arts to studying.

Sudhodhana hoped that his son would be content with his princely life and would never wish to leave to become a monk. He built his son three palaces, one for each season: hot, cold, and wet. Everyone who served Siddhartha was young and beautiful. Siddhartha traveled from palace to palace in an enclosed carriage, never seeing the outside world. He didn't think this was strange because he believed that everyone else lived as he did.

When Siddhartha was 16 years old, his father held a grand banquet at his palace to which he invited all the young women of the city. During the banquet, Siddhartha fell in love with the beautiful Yasodhara.

Yasodhara's father insisted that Siddhartha agree to a contest, a contest he would have to win before he could marry Yasodhara.

The first part of the contest was in art and literature. Siddhartha fluently recited 64 religious verses, easily outperforming the other contestants. The second part was in mathematics, and Siddhartha answered every question correctly. The third part was a test of physical strength. Siddhartha threw every opponent to the ground; no one could beat him. The final part was in archery, but Siddhartha broke every bow until his father brought him a large, heavy bow from the temple. Then, Siddhartha's arrow flew farther than all the rest.

After winning the contest, Siddhartha celebrated his marriage to Yasodhara in a ceremony that lasted ten days and nights.

Siddhartha lived a life of complete contentment. One day, while in the garden, he noticed the gardener at work, weeding the flowerbeds and transplanting new seedlings. Curious, he asked the gardener what he was doing.

The gardener replied, "The Maharajah likes the plants to be replaced before the flowers die." "Die? What does that mean?" asked Siddhartha.

The gardener gave a quick laugh; he had no way to explain to the prince the meaning of death. This laugh, like a stone thrown into a pond, disturbed Siddhartha for a moment, but he soon forgot about it.

Some time later, a singer came to perform for Siddhartha. She sang beautifully, but a note of sadness was in her voice. Siddhartha felt there was something odd about her song. But he had never encountered sadness, so he did not recognize what it was. He asked her about the song.

The singer replied, "It is a song about my homeland. I feel very homesick every time I sing it."

Siddhartha began to wonder what the rest of the world was like. He thought, "Are there places more lovely than this? Why have I never thought of venturing outside these walls?" So Siddhartha went to his father and told him of his wish to see the outside world. His father had expected this and was prepared.

He ordered that all the old, sick, and poor people be rounded up and removed from the area where Siddhartha would travel. On his 29th birthday, Siddhartha went outside the palace gates for the first time. He was riding in a litter carried by 36 men, and he had with him his beloved white horse, Kanthaka, and his favorite servant, Chandaka.

Everywhere he went, Siddhartha saw freshly painted houses and beautifully dressed people, who were happy and healthy. They showered him with rose petals and called out his name. He was delighted. He had no idea that his father had carefully arranged everything he saw.

Then, just as he was about to return to the palace, he caught a glimpse of two strange creatures down a narrow alley to his left. They were shaped like human beings, but they were so stooped that their backs seemed broken. What's more, their hair was white and sparse, their skin spotted and scarred, their bones protruded dreadfully, and they had lost most of their teeth.

Siddhartha asked Chandaka, "What are those creatures?"

"People!" replied Chandaka. "People like us."

"People? Really? Then why do they look like that?" asked Siddhartha.

"They are old, your Highness."

"What is old?"

"As the years go by, people get older and older. They lose their beauty, strength, and memory. It is something that happens to everyone. No one escapes," Chandaka explained.

Siddhartha thought, "People get old. Flowers die." Deeply disturbed, he silently returned to the palace.

The young prince couldn't ignore the uneasiness growing in his mind. Not long after this, he left the palace again, riding his white horse with Chandaka beside him. Soon they came across a woman coughing uncontrollably and spitting blood.

Terribly shocked, Siddhartha asked Chandaka, "What is wrong with her?"

"She is ill and in pain," replied Chandaka. "Ill" was another new word for Siddhartha.

Next, they came upon some men carrying a corpse on a stretcher. Their horses reared in alarm. "What is that?" Siddhartha asked Chandaka.

"Your Highness, it is better if you don't know," replied the loyal servant. "Tell me!" Siddhartha demanded angrily. "I order you!"

Chandaka had no choice. He drew Siddhartha to the side of the road, where many bodies wrapped in white cloth were lying on wooden stretchers. A fire had been lit and was beginning to consume the bodies.

"This is death, your Highness," Chandaka said. "Death is what separates us from our families. With death, we disappear from the world. It brings an end to life."

"Does everyone die?" asked Siddhartha softly. "Even a maharajah?"

"Yes," replied Chandaka, "everyone. Maharajahs, princes, princesses, farmers, and beggars: everyone will die."

Music greeted Siddhartha on his return to the palace. His wife had given birth to a son, and everyone was celebrating. But Siddhartha had no heart for the celebration. The door to real life had just opened for him.

The pain and terror that lay beyond haunted him like a nightmare that wouldn't go away.

Late that night, Siddhartha woke with the moon shining brightly. He thought if he could not unravel the mystery of this life of beauty and suffering, he would never be happy again. So he decided to leave his loved ones, his children, his wife, and his father. This was the first difficult decision Siddhartha had ever had to make.

But he knew that if he didn't leave, he would spend his life trapped in an artificial world.

Siddhartha woke the loyal Chandaka, muffled the hooves of his horse with straw, and quietly left his home.

"Chandaka, thank you for staying with me for such a long time," Siddhartha said. "Now, it's time to say goodbye. Go home to my father and my wife. Tell them I will not return until I have found a way to end the suffering of life and death."

With tears in his eyes, Chandaka cried, "If you leave, won't the princess and your father be terribly sad? Who will teach your son? How can you not care about leaving them?"

Siddhartha replied, "That's why I want to find a way to rid the world of pain. Happiness and love seem but a brief dream. We can't help but be separated from those we love when we die. I want to save people from suffering. If I succeed, I will return to the palace." Then, Siddhartha drew his gilded sword and cut off his hair.

After this, Siddhartha saw five naked men sitting on the river bank.

They had rejected all worldly comforts and would stay where they were until they found enlightenment. Siddhartha walked into the grove and joined the the five monks. For more than six years, he stayed there without uttering a word. He drank only rainwater and ate but a little wild food. His skin hung on his bones, but his spirit remained strong.

One morning, he heard the sound of music. A bamboo raft was floating downstream, and on it sat an old man playing a flute and a young man playing a seven-stringed lute. Suddenly, the old man stopped playing and spoke to the younger man. "Don't tune the strings too tightly or they will break. If they are too loose, the lute won't play. Find the middle way." These words rung in Siddhartha's ears like the clang of a bell. He crawled to his feet, slowly entered the river, and washed the dirt from his body.

A kindly young woman passing by offered him a bowl of rice gruel. He ate a few mouthfuls before calling to the five monks, "Come and eat with me. If you tune the strings too tightly, they will break."

The five monks, believing he had given in to physical desire, angrily turned their backs and walked away.

Siddhartha smiled. He knew he had made the same mistake the monks were making. He sat down and began to meditate under a large tree. He needed to rethink everything, to find a new path to the truth.

As he meditated, many strange images came into his mind: evil spirits wild beasts, and beautiful women.

Siddhartha struggled to quiet his mind. He opened his eyes and looked at the stars. One by one, they began to disappear. His "self" disappeared with them. Everything was emptiness. All thought, desire, and suffering vanished. With this discovery, he became Buddha, the enlightened one.

Now that he knew this truth, Buddha wondered if he should tell others what he had learned. It wasn't easy to grasp. Could he help others understand it? He decided he must become like a boat that would carry humanity across the great river of suffering. So he went to the five monks and told them of the truth he had experienced. They became his followers, and Buddha embarked on his task of bringing enlightenment to the people, a task that would last for 45 years.

In Buddha's time, society in India was divided into four castes, with the lords and warriors at the top, followed by the priests, then the farmers and merchants, and at the bottom, the untouchables. Caste was inherited, passed on from one generation to the next. There was no possibility of change or movement. The caste system was supported by India's religious beliefs. Only the top three castes were allowed to read the Hindu scriptures.

The untouchables were not permitted to know anything about the scriptures. Anyone who taught the untouchables such things was severely punished.

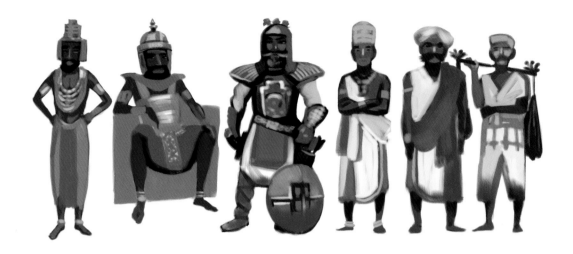

Buddha wanted to show people another way to live. He believed all people were equal and that there should be no caste system, no divisions in society. He even instructed his followers to help everyone find enlightenment and not merely to seek their own. He gave spiritual guidance to everyone, no matter what rank or caste. Buddha preached to all and accepted gifts from everyone.

Buddha used very clever methods of explaining the truth to his listeners. For example, a woman came to him, weeping because her son had died. She sobbed, "I must have my son back or I will die."

He merely smiled at her and said, "Go to the village and find a household in which no one has died. Ask them for some mustard seeds. Then, bring me the seeds, and I will release you from your suffering."

The woman searched the entire village. Although everyone was happy to give her some mustard seeds, she found no one whom death had not touched. So the woman returned to Buddha and knelt before him, saying, "I understand. I won't try to bring my son back to life. Death comes to all of us. I see that now. Teach me, Master, teach me to understand the truth of existence."

On another occasion, Buddha came across a man preparing to slaughter a lamb as a sacrifice to the gods. He said to the man, "If you are grateful to the gods for being good to you, you ought to offer your own life in sacrifice. What has the lamb got to do with it? Why do you wish to make it suffer so miserably?"

The man replied with words from the Hindu scriptures: "Our sacred books say that if a life is sacrificed to the gods, its soul will go to heaven. I am not making the lamb suffer. I am helping it get to heaven."

Buddha replied, "So why not kill your father or your mother or yourself? Why miss such a wonderful opportunity to get to heaven? The lamb may not even want to go to heaven."

The man put down his knife and said to Buddha, "You have awakened me. You have made me see the error of my ways."

Buddha accepted many followers or disciples. He saw them as seeds, seeds of enlightenment. Before he died, his last words were: "Remember, each and everyone of you is a Buddha." He believed that everyone could become an "enlightened one," and that he had simply set the wheel of the world in motion. The wheel would not stop when he died. There would be others to keep it turning.

Many thousands of people respected Buddha and followed his teachings, but there were others who disliked him and what he taught. The lords, priests, and merchants did everything they could to destroy his teachings about equality, so they could preserve the ancient system of castes.

Even so, Buddha's teachings flourished. His ideas crossed the mountains, into China, then into Japan, Tibet, and Southeast Asia. Today, Buddhism is one of the most widely practiced religions in the world. Throughout the ages, those who have attained enlightenment have continued to pass down Buddha's truth.

BIOGRAPHY

Author Anna Carew-Miller is a freelance writer and former teacher, who lives in rural northwestern Connecticut with her husband and daughter. Although she has a Ph.D. in American Literature and has done extensive research and writing on literary topics, more recently, Anna has written books for younger readers, including reference books and middle reader mysteries.